When God Speaks, Obey!

When God Speaks, Obey!

We all have a testimony; we all have a story.
We should share it because we never know who needs to hear it!

By

CARROLL MORGAN

ARPress
ILLUMINATING IDEAS.
EMPOWERING VOICES.

ARPress
45 Dan Road Suite 36
Canton MA 02021

| Hotline: | 1(888) 821-0229 |
| Fax: | 1(508) 545-7580 |

Ordering Information:
Quantity Sales. Special discounts are available on quantity purchases by corporations, associations, and others. For details, contact the publisher at the address above.

Printed in the United States of America.

| ISBN-13 | Paperback | 979-8-89356-564-5 |
| | eBook | 979-8-89356-565-2 |

Library of Congress Control Number: 2024903092

And we know that in all things God works for the good of those who love him, who have been called according to his purpose. (Rom. 8:28, NIV)

For I have learned to be content whatever the – circumstance, I know what it is to be in need and I know what it is to have plenty I have learned the secret of being content in any and every situation, whether well fed or hungry, whether living in plenty or in want. I can do all this through him who gives me strength. (Phil. 4:11–13)

Contents

PREFACE

This story begins Halloween night October 31, 1951 in the small southwest Louisiana town of Crowley. The city would have a Halloween party at the local football stadium for all the youth of Crowley between ages ten and fifteen. I was an impressible youth of twelve who had just a week before played his first football game on this field scoring a touchdown. They had a bicycle safety day, the Chief of Police Maxwell "Maxie" Barousse who was in his dress uniform, made such an impression on me. From his dress and speech, from that time on, I always wanted to be a policeman like Chief Barousse. I didn't know then how close I would come to being just like him.

My early childhood, I was raised Methodist by two great Christian parents, Edison Elwin "Eddie" and Leona Morgan. One of my uncles by marriage, two first cousins, and my brother were all Methodist ministers. Alone, with a support group of true Christian sisters; Verdie Morgan Jones, Betty Morgan Steele, brother Eddie Jr., aunts, uncles, and first cousins. I don't remember any bad memories of my childhood.

One of my favorite growing up story is in 1954, a childhood friend J. W. "Bill" Stanton and I went to Shreveport to visit our brothers who were attending Centenary College in Shreveport. That was when the University of Arkansas and LSU would play their football game in the old fairground stadium in Shreveport. We got to see our first LSU football game that Saturday afternoon for $ 6.00 (I'm still a diehard LSU fan) and Elvis Presley for a $1.25 on the Louisiana Hayride that Saturday night.

I knew Jesus all my life, but at about the age of fifteen, I started drinking and smoking cigarettes and started on a thirty-year journey of some great accomplishments and some great disappointments caused by the alcoholism that took control at times.

I was a fair to good football player. I had some offers from a few Jr. Colleges and a walk on from Southwestern Louisiana Institute, (SLI) which is now the University of Louisiana at Lafayette. I decided that I would rather go to Centenary College, a Methodist college in Shreveport hoping to get a change and to stop drinking.

That didn't work out to good because the week of finals, five of us got five fifths of White Port wine at $.75 a fifth. We got into a bit of trouble and were asked to leave the campus voluntarily. We could keep the grades that we had made up to that point. Instead of letting my parents know how stupid their son was I resigned and decided to stay with some friends until the semester was over.

That spring I told my parents that I wanted to try to pick up a football scholarship at SLI. I had talked to the coach and he had said I could walk on. Well I was there for about a month and I was so out of shape that they were killing me on the football field. One afternoon a friend from Crowley Mike Johnson and I were sitting in the student union drinking a coke when another friend from Crowley, who was a football player at Texas A&M, came in. We started talking. He said he was tired of playing football at A&M and was going to join the army. He asks me and Mike if we wanted to join the army with him. We discussed it and went to the recruiting office. They told us to come back in the morning to take some test. That was the last time we saw that friend from A&M. He went back and made all Southwest Conference at Halfback. Mike and I joined the army and were sent to Fort Chaffee, Arkansas.

The week before we left for Fort Chaffee, I was invited to a swim party with some old friends. At the party was a beautiful green eyed blonde, Linda Dell Wilmoth, who I had known casually from going

Linda Wilmoth Morgan (August 21, 1940–December 31, 2003).

Carroll Morgan 1957

to church and school with her. I had graduated from high school with her sister, Alice. Linda was a year behind me. I had never really paid any attention to her before but that night we just clicked.

While at Fort Chaffee, I caught pneumonia and was delayed a week from finishing basic. That gave her time to graduate from high school so she came with my parent to graduation from basic. After basic training, I got two weeks leave and most of it was spent with her. By the time, I was to report back to the army I was madly in love. I was stationed at Fort Rucker, Alabama. Being away from her didn't help. I started drinking harder; until one night in July, I got drunk and drove a borrowed car off the road into a forty-foot deep rock quarry. I was unconscious for five days. They sent a telegram to my daddy that I probably would not be alive when they got to Fort Rucker. That was one of many miracles that God has performed in my life.

Because I had missed so many days of school, they set me back; and I had to wait for another class to begin. I was lonesome, lovesick, and a con man so I kept trying to get out of the army until finally they gave me a General Discharge under Honorable Conditions. I left the army in October of 1958 in time to enroll at McNeese State College in Lake Charles with the girl that occupied most of my thoughts. It didn't take but a month until February 3, 1959 we rode over to Hardin County, Texas and eloped. We were married by a Methodist Preacher in Kountze, Texas.

We didn't tell anyone because Linda wanted to complete the semester. In the meantime, she gets pregnant for our first son Kent Douglas. He was born January 17, 1960.

At that time, I was working as assistant manager at an office supply store for $30.00 a week. Well, when we told her parents, you can imagine that they weren't to thrill about us bringing a child into the world on $30.00 a week. Her father, who was district manager for United Gas Pipe Line, got me a job with the pipeline in Westlake, LA making $300.00 a month. He also bought us a 1953 Plymouth car.

We were doing great until someone pointed out that family members couldn't work under the supervision of another family member. So, I was transferred to Gulfport, Mississippi where Kent

Douglas was born, January 17, 1960 and a little over a year later our daughter, Jenifer Elaine, was born February 26, 1961.

I controlled my drinking during the week, but on the weekend, I would go on binges. I was drinking up more money than I was making so I started borrowing from loan companies. This went on for about a year until the loan companies started calling United Gas Pipe Line. One-week end, when we came back to visit Linda's family in Lafayette, Louisiana, her father talked to me about it. He asks me what I would do without him. I told him I would show him as soon as I could get back to Gulfport. I went back to Gulfport quit my job. Picked up a wife and two young children and went to Houston, Texas. I had a second cousin there who said he could find me a job. He did, selling vacuum cleaners. I didn't sell any; the '53 Plymouth broke down. I had to call daddy to tow it back to Crowley.

I had been unemployed for about four weeks, living at home with my parents and a wife and two small children; one one-year-old, and one, a little over two years old.

I had taken the municipal police officers civil service test and at the time had made the highest score of ninety-nine out of one hundred. On September 14, 1962, my father came in for lunch and asks me if I still wanted to be a policeman. I told him sure. He told me to talk to a city councilman, Howard Duncan. I did that afternoon. Mr. Duncan called seven councilmen and then Mayor Joe Gielen on the phone and got them to commit to vote for me. He told me to go to work Monday morning.

I went to work Monday morning September 17, 1962, where I reported to the Chief of Police, Maxie Barousse. He told me he didn't know anything about me being hired but that he was glad to have me. The same Chief of Police that had impressed me so much as a twelve-year-old.

This beginning of a twenty-four-year career that took me from a parking meter police officer, up through the ranks to Major with the Crowley Police Department then to Chief of Police of Jennings and a ten-year career with the Louisiana Department of Corrections, for a total of thirty-four years of law enforcement experience.

The rest of the story will be about my rise through the ranks with some of the more interesting cases that I have worked. How God took an alcoholic, cleaned him up, and made him Chief of Police.

Hopefully this essay will show that you never know who you may affect by your dress and speech. How God's grace works. That when you accept the Lordship of Jesus Christ and make him the focal point of who you are he will forgive you, clean you up and give you "the desires of your heart."

The road has not always been smooth, but the one consistent thing is that God has never forsaken me nor left me. His Grace has been there through the triumphs and the pain.

I dedicate this book to the God of Abraham, Isaac, and Jacob; and to the Son of God, Jesus my Savior and Lord.

CHAPTER 1

The Crowley Years

Train up a child in the way he should go: and when
he is old, he will not depart from it. (Prov. 22:6)

September 17th, 1962 I reported to work to start my career as a
policeman. Boy I was so proud, I know I set a record for writing
parking tickets, I was so dedicated to be the very best I could be. I
was so good that one of the riches businessmen in Crowley told me
that because of my dedication that if I ever wanted another job to
come to him that he would hire me in a heartbeat. To tell the truth,
I don't think the passion for being a policeman ever wore off. I still
get excited about cases that I see in the news and speculate about
how they should be investigated. I have fun but drive other people
batty.

Picture of Carroll Morgan taken in 1962

I worked for about three months as a parking meter patrolman working every other Saturday and every other Sunday as a dispatcher; forty-eight hours a week for $300.00 a month. I would go back after I would eat supper and ride with the shift supervisors from around seven to ten in the evening to get experience on regular patrol. I learned a lot about how to police and to treat people from such officers as Captain Joseph "Joe" Meche, his brother Lieutenant "Greasy" Meche, Lieutenant "Black" Herpin, Sgt. Dudley Hoffpauir, Patrolman Frist Class Harry Shreve, Patrolman Joseph "Barney" Leleux, and our two Black- American Patrolmen George "Mr." Carrier and Robert "Bo-Diddley) Scott.

Captain Meche oversaw detectives, I think he was the only one. He taught me about investigations. He taught me how to cultivate and protect informants. He taught me how to lift and to take fingerprints; although in twenty-four years, I never solved a case by using fingerprints. He was as serious as a heart attack but was a very good trainer.

Captain Meche's brother Lieutenant Meche was the exact opposite. He was a prankster. He was an ex-boxer, wrestler who would tell you all about his exploits, but he knew people and how to handle them. I learn a lot of street smarts from him.

Lieutenant George "Black" Herpin, by the time I got on the police department, he had been put on desk duty. He had survived a police shooting where he and his partner patrolman, Ezra "Bubba" Foreman, were shot answering a domestic disturbance call. They were both shot with a 12 gauge shotgun as they walked up to the house. Bubba Foreman was fatally wounded and Lieutenant Herpin was shot in the side and arm. He taught me about dispatching and office procedure. He also was such a gentle and kind person that he would explain all the other officers' quirks. He would explain the reason some were easy to get along with and others not so easy.

Sergeant Dudley Hoffpauir taught me self-confidence. He reinforced what my father had always taught; when you say, something mean it. He taught me that you only told a subject one time what you wanted done, if they didn't comply with a lawful command then you arrested them. After a few times the word gets out that you are a no nonsense policeman. He taught that you are to be taken seriously or risk things getting out of hand.

Patrolman First Class Harry Shreve wasn't around long because he died of a brain aneurism about a year after I became a policeman, but in the short time I knew him, he taught me how to be laid back and not to take myself to seriously. He was always smiling and telling you a joke. Earlier before I became a policeman and when I was dating Linda, we had parked on a gravel road right up from Harry's house on West Hutchinson. When we got ready to leave, somehow, the car slipped into a ditch and we couldn't get out so we walked to Harry's house; and he came with his truck and chain and he pulled us out of the ditch. No one ever knew and I was always grateful to him.

Patrolman Joseph "Barney" Leleux got a bad rap because of his resemblance to the TV character, Barney Fife. Joe was much more serious and a good police officer. He taught me how to take criticism and turn it into a joke about yourself. He taught me how to really laugh at myself. I can do things that make me an unwittingly comedian I will always be thankful to him for helping me to put my ego into my back pocket and sitting on it.

3

Because they meant so much to me and my family, I will always refer to Patrolmen George Carrier and Robert Scott as Mr. Carrier and Mr. Robert or Bo-Diddley. Of all the people that I have policed with I have never felt safer then when I was with Mr. Carrier and Bo-Diddley. We had a true trust of each other. Each knew we had each other's backs.

Mr. Carrier was an avid domino's player. I always thought I was good because I had been playing since I was about twelve with my father and uncles every Saturday night. Mr. Carrier and I must have played three hundred games and he may have let me win two.

He and Bo taught me not to be intimidated by race. They taught me to treat everyone the same. They taught me to expect the same out of everyone. They believed that the law was colored blind even though the first four years that I was there, under Chief Barousse, they worked the same shift six in the evening to two in the morning and they could only work the Black/American section of town. Crowley was still adjusting to integration. When Chief John "Al" Gibson became chief he changed that. He put them on a regular shift and they could patrol all over Crowley. Chief Gibson also hired three more Black/American patrolmen and the first five women two of whom were black on the Crowley Police force.

I completed forty lecture hours for four Credit Units for the 5th LSU Basic Training for Recruits in 1962 that was held at the Iberia Parish Sheriff 's office. It was sponsored by then Iberia Parish, Sheriff Jerry Whatteny. A retired FBI agent, Skipper Martin, was the head instructor. We were taught report writing, traffic investigations, court testimony, fire arm safety, and qualification and some basic defensive tactics.

I went on patrol the first of 1963. I would work my regular shift five days a week and then on one of the weekend days, I would work as a dispatcher. Everyone worked a forty-eight-hour week, this was in the days, that if you were working the graveyard shift, ten in the-evening to six in the morning, you may be the only one on patrol. For the first two years, from 1962 until 1964, the Acadia Parish Sheriff 's office closed at midnight and the State Police had a parish trooper, who only worked days or when he was called out for a major

4

accident. Now, six days a week you would have at least one other officer, either Mr. Carrier or Bo-diddly up until two in the morning.

Patrolman Robert "Bo Diddly"
Scott Patrolman George "Mr." Carrier

I must put in here that by the time I got onto the police force Chief Barousse was a serious alcoholic.

During the four years under Chief Barousse, there were many serious and humorous things that happened. On the serious side was the first incident with an African-American female who had run a stop sign. I wrote her a ticket. At that time, we could allow them to sign the ticket to promise that they would show within five days to post a bond and get a court date. She refused to sign the ticket; and after several minutes of going back and forth with her, I made the mistake of telling her "if she didn't sign the ticket, I was going to jerk her black ass out of the car and arrest her." She signed the ticket but beat me back to the police station and I received a radio call to report to the Chief's office.

After Chief Barousse got through telling me in no uncertain terms that what I had said and done wasn't going to be tolerated, he got in the patrol car with me. For the next two days, he and I worked traffic together. He taught me that when I approached the driver, to tell them why they were being stopped, I would say, "May I please have your driver's license?" and tell them thank you. I would then walk back to my unit, write the ticket, go back to their car, and ask them to please sign this ticket. It does not admit guilt, it only promise to appear to post bond and to get a court date.

Since that time, I have never had to go court to testify on a traffic ticket. They all pled guilty. I never wrote a lot of traffic, because I must confess that at that time, I did like to speed and I didn't want to be a hypocrite. It had to be a serious violation or a probable cause situation for me to stop you for a traffic violation.

Another serious incident was one of the freedom rider buses came through and they were supposed to stop at the bus station on Third Street and Ave. E. There was one problem, the KKK were inside the bus station waiting on the freedom riders. Chief Barousse came up with the idea of letting the Klan go inside the bus station; and as soon as they did, we all drove up got out with our shot guns and encircled the bus station. We wouldn't let the Klan out or anyone else in. When the freedom bus arrived, Chief Barousse got on it and told the bus driver that the bus station was closed to keep on traveling. We let the Klan out of the bus station thirty minutes later.

The last major incident under Chief Barousse was one Friday night in late 1965. We went into a predominantly black bar. There was an ordinance that said a bar had to be lit up enough so that you could clearly see faces. We had been getting complaints about this place of underage drinking and prostitution so Chief Barousse and the whole shift which was about five of us that night went in. Chief Barousse told the owner to turn all the lights on in the bar and to leave them on. We then check for underage drinkers. As we were leaving, we didn't get on to the sidewalk good before the owner turned the lights back off. Chief Barousse lost his cool and went back in the bar grabbed the owner by his belt and the back of his neck and as he went out the door. Chief Barousse kicked him in the rear and he landed in the middle of the street.

Because of the advanced alcoholism and this incident, the City Council held a hearing; and although Chief Barousse was an elected official, he was forced to retire early in 1965.

Chief Maxwell Barrousse
Chief of Police, Crowley, Louisiana
1948 - 1966

There was an encounter one Saturday afternoon at the A&P grocery store. We had gotten a complaint from the dispatcher that a woman had pulled a pistol on another woman in the parking lot at the A & P store. Lieutenant Vernon Gauthreaux and I answered the call. As we approached the woman who fit the description, she began to reach her hand into her purse, I ordered her not to put her hand into her purse but she did not reply to the command. She reached into her purse and came out with a small 25 cal. semi-automatic pistol. I was too close to her to draw my weapon. My choices were either try to hit her hard enough to dislodge the weapon from her hand or try to take it away from her. I chose the latter; and when I reached to grab her hand, I was just fast enough to get a little part of the barrel and could take it from her.

I never thought of being frighten until I sat down to write the report. I began to shake like a leaf in a hurricane. We got a call one evening to go to a house, that a man had shot at his girlfriend and he was in a bedroom trying to reload the gun. When we got to the house and Sergeant Magnon and another officer were talking to him through an open door into the bedroom. When I got there, I began to negotiate with him to drop the gun and to surrender. As I was talking to him, I could see into the bullet receiver. I saw that they were all empty, so I moved slowly into the bedroom and I acted like I was going to sit to talk to him. When I saw him take his eyes off me for a second and look toward Sgt. Magnon, I rushed him and pushed him halfway through an opened window where the gun fell to the ground. When we found the gun, it had jammed with the hammer half back so that he couldn't open the chamber to reload the gun.

Now, for a few humorous incidents, but kind of sad, that occurred. Early in 1963, Chief Barousse asked me to drive him to a Chiefs of Police meeting in Alexandria, LA. He stayed sober all morning during the meeting; but at lunch, he and other chiefs started drinking right before, during, and after lunch; and he got drunk. He decided that he didn't want to go home drunk and that we would spend the night in Alexandria. I got a room for us with two beds at the old Bentley Hotel in downtown Alexandria. I got him settled into his room. I went down stairs to eat supper and to call Linda to tell her that he wanted to spend the night. I hadn't really started back to drinking yet, so I was sober. I went back to the room after supper and after talking to my wife Linda. Chief Barousse had urinated in his bed and had gotten into mine. I had to get another room for me. I was not a happy camper.

All these stories happened at night. I was searching a bag factory building where a door had been left open. As I was searching the area, a time clock clicked and sounded just like the hammer of a pistol cocking, I swirled around expecting to see an armed assailant and almost shot a time clock. No shots fired.

I was working as a detective. I got a radio call to be on the look-out for a certain vehicle with three white males who were wanted for armed robbery. I spotted that car at a car wash and I called for backup. Before the backup could get there, the suspects started to leave, I blocked them with my unmarked unit. I open my door, put my shotgun on it, got them out of their car, and told them to come to my unit and to put their hands on the hood. When they did, I started to walk away from my unit to get behind them. I had forgotten to put the car in park and when I took my foot off the brake, the car started to move forward slowly. They held it back long enough for me to get the car into park. When the backup came, one of the officers, who was patting them down, got a surprise. One of the suspects had gotten so frighten that he had defecated on himself

We received a domestic call that a male suspect was beating his wife. When we got there, the suspect was about 6'4" and weighted about 300 lbs. My partner, James Magnon, and I had placed the male under arrest for disturbing the peace by threating to beat his wife. When we went to cuff him, he started to resist. My partner weight about 140 soaking wet. James had hold of one of his arms and I had the other, and we were trying to get them behind him to cuff him. He was picking James off the floor and slamming him into me.

We finally got his arms behind him and when we tried putting the cuffs on him, his wrist was too big. The handcuffs didn't fit around his wrist. (That was before flexible hand cuffs). I told James to turn him loose and I did at the same time.

I then used the old cliché, I told him "You have two choices. One, you can get into the back seat of the car or I can call an ambulance because I'm going to have to hurt you."

He put his hands over his head and told me, "Mr. Morgan, I'm not mad at you. I'm just mad at my wife. I'm sorry. I'll get in the car." He did and we didn't ever have any more trouble out of him.

Although Chief Barousse was an alcoholic and did some very questionable things, deep inside, he was a truly good man who really cared about the people of Crowley. He knew how to handle people. He could arrest you for capital murder and you knew you were going to get the death sentence, but you felt sorry for him because he had to arrest you.

In the short time I served under him, I learned more about how to handle the street and the proper way to police. The job of a policeman is to be a servant. The people pay your salary. That you must be firm but fair. I learned that it takes five years to become a patrol officer

In 1963, I attended fifty-one lecture hours of the LSU in Service Principle of Law Enforcement III for 5.1 credit units. In 1963, I was promoted to Patrolman 1sat Class, I made a ninety-seven on the civil service test.

Captain Willie Spell was appointed interim Chief of Police. He served for about six months until the next election in 1965. Chief Spell was a good man, but because he had been on the force for twenty years under Chief Barousse, the city wanted a change and voted him out and elected Chief John "Al" Gibson. In 1964, I was promoted to Sergeant I, and made a ninety-seven on The Civil Service test.

Chief Gipson brought some more progressive ideas when he became Chief of Police. Because of the civil rights movements, almost every city in the south was feeling the tension between the races. So, in September of 1965, I went to forty Lecture Hours, four Credits units, and a Mob and Riot Control seminar at LSU put on by the FBI. When I came back, I organized and took command of a Tactical Unit. We trained twice a month on a weekend. We had about three weeks of unrest in the Black-American community, we had a few loud mouths that we took away in a hurry and defused most of the crowds. It never really got out of hand. By this time, I had been promoted to Lieutenant. I made a ninety-six on the civil service test. It was during this time that Chief Gibson had hired three more Black-American policemen and the first five female officers two of whom were Black-Americans. The female officers were used as dispatchers and secretaries. The whole time I worked at the Crowley Police Department we never had any patrol women.

The way that we brought the crowds under control, I asked for five volunteers to work the graveyard shift (ten in the evening to six in the morning) with me. They were three Black-Americans officers, Mr. Carrier, Bo Diddly, and Alvin "Boo Boo" Caesar. Lieutenant Paul Laverne and Sergeant James Magnon were the other two officers. I broke the city up into three Zones: North East Crowley, South Crowley, and West Crowley. I put Lieutenant Laverne in the Northeast zone; Officer Caesar in the South Zone and in the trouble zone; and in the West Zone, I put Mr. Carrier, Bo Diddley, and Sergeant Magnon. If there was a call in one of the other zones, Sergeant Magnon was sent as the backup officer. I also patrolled and covered all calls in every zone.

What made this successful was the saturation of all the zones with a police unit. We had a patrol unit in front of the bars on Highway ninety every two to three minutes. As one unit, would turn off ninety to go into the other parts of the West Zone, and another unit would be coming down Highway ninety. By twelve o'clock, there was no one left on the streets.

When the community settled down, we took the same concept into any high incident areas. We would saturate patrol at any zones that were troublesome in the area until we got them under control. The greatest crime deterrent is some heavy police presence that is courteous, fair, and firm. The people in the high crime must know that you are going to protect them, but that you are only going to use the force necessary to get the job done.

After we would get the area under control, I would send a community resource officer in to get out of the patrol unit and walk among the residents to make personal relationships with them. If they had any police problems or ever needed something, they had someone who knew them. I would keep this resource officer in the same area for about a month. Then he would do periodic checks about once a week.

From January 12 to January 16, 1970 I attended the LSU Traffic School with forty lecture hours and 4four credits. I learned how to reconstruct an accident scene and how to tell how fast a vehicle was traveling by skid marks. It was probably the only school that I didn't ever apply what I learned because I never worked traffic my whole career. I may have investigated two to three accidents in my entire career. I only stayed a patrolman for a year and most of that was in dispatching.

In September of 1971, I attended the first LSU Juvenile Officers School that was twelve weeks or 464 lecture hours for 46.4 Credits. I tied for second in the class half a point away from the first place finisher. While there, I was promoted to Captain. I made a ninety-five on the civil service test.

I went back to Crowley and took over all the investigation secton. I was still commander of the tactical unit and hostage negotiator. During the election of 1974, a retired State Police Lieutenant, Allen Castille, won for the Chief of Police. There wasn't much change to operations. Chief Castille wanted to promote me to major because he didn't believe in Assistant Chiefs. I took the civil service exam and was promoted to Major in 1976. I made a ninety on the civil service test.

My drinking had become more profound during this time because I could name my shift. I could come in whenever I wanted to. I had run and won for treasurer of the Crowley Municipal Police Association.

I had run in 1974 for Sergeant at Arms for the Louisiana Municipal Police Officers Association (MPOA) and had won. In 1976, the president-elect resigned. I had been vice president at the time, so I ascended to the Presidency.

During that time, I increased the membership in the MPOA from 950 to over 1500 members. Another Crowley police officer, Joey Reddlich, and I went to every city in Louisiana that had a police department and signed up members.

Through a raffle for a new car and new membership dues, the MPOA went from having $900.00 in the bank to having over $10,000.00 in the bank after all expenses had been paid for my-convention. This was due mainly because of the arrangement that Major Huey "Joe" Sexton and his wife, Barbara, had with the motel and some of the businesses in Lake Charles with Joey Reddlich and his wife Janet, and Major Charles Baxley. Baton Rouge police helped me recruit new members and sold tickets; and a special thanks for the help of Dick Belson and his son, Art Belson, and all the employees of Belsco Uniform and Gun Store from Lafayette by furnishing all the personnel, food, and beverages for the hospitality room. The convention was in March 1977 in Lake Charles, Louisiana.

CHAPTER 2

The Downfall

For the wages of sin is death, but the gift of God
is eternal life in Christ Jesus our Lord. (Rom. 6:23,
NIV)

During this time, there were some very good things that I got
accomplished. I had risen to the rank of Major, the highest rank
under the Chief of Police that I could attain. I am the only officer
to obtain the rank of Major in the Crowley Police Department. I
helped form a tac- tical unit. I attended the first Juvenile Officers
Institute in Louisiana was tied for second in a class of twenty-five.
That class produced one Chief Deputy, Mike Barnett; East Baton
Rouge Parish Sheriff 's office; two Chiefs of Police, Kenneth Lewis;
Shreveport, Louisiana Police Department; and me, Chief of Police
of Jennings, Louisiana. I attended the first Hostage Negotiation
School held in Louisiana. My son, Louisiana State Police Sergeant,
Tracy Morgan, is now the Instructor for the State Police and police
departments all over the United States and Canada. I was elected
President of the Louisiana Municipal Police Officers Association
(MPOA). I was chairman of the legislative committee. I help formed
a coalition between the Fire Union, the Police union, the MPOA, the
Chiefs Association, the Fraternal Order of Police, and the Sheriff 's
Association to help get part of the lottery dedicated to the Police and
Fire supplemental pay.

Edwin Edwards, who was Governor at the time, remarked that he
was highly impressed that we could all come together.

I instituted zone and saturated patrolling in Crowley. Lieutenant Cecil Moore and I wrote up the first mock Bank robbery and hostage taking in a real bank setting on a weekend when the bank was closed. We were highly praised by the LSU Police Training faculty and the FBI for the success of the project.

I was involved in several big investigations with Region Three Investigators, Lieutenant Louis Ackel, Sgt. Harry Courville, Sgt. Ferdie Miller, and Trooper Donald Stutes of the Louisiana State Police stationed in Lafayette.

I was blessed to have met several well-known politicians, who, in some way, each had an influence on my career. Governor Edwin Edwards, who was my first attorney, helped with a lot of legislationon to benefit policemen. Though there are many negative reports about him, I can honestly say that the governor never once lied to me or led me to believe he would help me when he couldn't. He even told me the truth when he could have said something else that would have benefited him. Congressman Peppers from Florida had a bill before Congress to exempt all police from the first $5,000.00 of their salaries. This was doing the run off for Governor with J. Bennett Johnston, the first-time Edwin Edward ran for Governor in 1972. At that time, he was a Congressman from the Louisiana 7th district. I met him at his office in Lake Charles. I told him about Congressman Pepper's bill and asked him to support it. He told me that he doesn't know anything about the bill, but as soon as he got back to Washington, he would consider it and let me know. He wrote me a letter about a week later explaining that he couldn't vote for the bill the way it was written, it had too many law enforcement people on it that didn't deserve the break. If Congressman Pepper would clean the bill up, he would support it.

Major Carroll Morgan, executive office of the Crowley Police Department, was appointed president of the 1200 member Municipal Police Officers Association, after Captain Chris Boudreaux resigned from that post. Major Morgan will be the host for the organization's convention next year in Crowley. (Post-Signal Staff Photo)

Senator Russell Long impressed me with his candor. I had the privilege to be his bodyguard. He was making a speech at the Rice Festival building on the Panama Canal treaty that would put the canal back under control of Panama. A controversial issue that he supported while most Louisiana voters were against it. I had brought him into Crowley for a speech in an unmarked car to the back of the Rice Festival building so that he could miss a crowd of about fifty to seventy-five protesters out front. I got him in and out without any incidents. As I was taking him back to his motel, he told the reasoning behind his vote and support. He was one of the most personable politicians that I ever met. He talked to you like he had known you forever. I must have made an impression on him because about a year later, he asked Judge Edmond Reggie, who was giving him a coffee reception to invite me and my wife Linda, that he wanted to see me. He even had the photographer to take a picture with him, Linda, and me.

Governor Charles "Buddy" Roemer was one of the smartest politicians that I have met. When you went in to see him, you had better know your subject because he was going to be well versed on it. If he thought you had thought a project through and you could convince him that you could make it work and could give him a source of funding, he would do as much as he could to help you with it with the legislature.

Governor Jimmie H. Davis had the best memory of anyone that I have known. If he ever met you, he knew who you were and under what circumstance that he had met you. I had met him one time at a music rehearsal in Shreveport. My roommate at Centenary College was his guitar player, so I had gone to the rehearsal with my roommate. This was in 1957 and I met him again in Crowley in 1962 and he knew who I was and where he had met me. I met him again in 1989 in Lake Arthur, he was in his nineties and he knew who I was.

I only met Senator J. Bennett Johnston once when he spoke to a Chief of Police meeting in Lafayette. He was very personable and was very interested in what everyone had to say.

I first met Senator Landrieu when she was the Louisiana State Treasurer. I had been trying to get the Jennings police department into the Louisiana Municipal Police Officers Retirement System. I had contacted everyone for help; the Social Security Administration, the Retirement System, the Louisiana Treasurer Department, and others. Everywhere I turned, the door seemed to be closed. Then after about three years of trying to find a way to get into the Retirement System, I got a call from one of the employee's in the treasurer's office wanting to know if we were a dry or wet parish. I told her we were a wet parish, one that sold alcoholic beverages. She said that because of that, we were mandated to be in the Louisiana Municipal Police Retirement System. I shall always be grateful to the Senator and her office when she was Louisiana Treasurer. The difference was that, the policeman retiring under the Municipal Retirement System got sixty percent of their salary after thirty years; while the policemen retiring under Municipal Police Retirement System got one hundred percent of their salary after thirty years.

US Senator John Breaux, when he was an aide to Governor Edwards, was a neighbor of mine in Crowley, he lived a block away from me. Senator Breaux was always helpful in getting things not only from Baton Rouge but also Washington DC.

Congressman Chris John, he was always helpful getting important legislation written up when he was a state representative. He also was helpful as a congressman.

Congressman Otto Passman; I only met him once. That was when he was put into the Hotel Deu Hospital in New Orleans, Louisiana. This is when he was under investigation for dealings that he had with the South Korean Tung Sung Parks. I was on detail to body guard him and some of his friends. We stayed at a hotel in New Orleans. He was highly paranoid about everything.

Dean Fritz McCameron was head of the LSU Extension Service, which covered Law Enforcement training. He was the very best friend the Police had for education, both through the Law Enforcement Academy, the LSU Basic Training, the LSU Traffic Institute, and the Juvenile Officers Institute. I and all other Louisiana Law Enforcement personnel owe Dean McCameron a great debt for his service to the Police. He always wanted input from the police themselves.

US Attorney General Janet Reno, I met her once at a meeting set up by US Attorney for the Western District of Louisiana Mike Skinner. She was a very gracious lady who gave a good speech.

Louisiana State Attorney General Jack Gremillion would come to the International Rice Festival every year that Chief Barousse was Chief of Police of Crowley. After the festival, they would go to State Senator Bill Cleveland's camp. He was very friendly and personable.

Secretary of State Fox McKeithen, very a good supporter and friend to Police. He would help get bills through the legislature. State Representative Jack Strain was a very good friend to police. He would author almost any bill that the police wanted pass.

During this time in early 1979, my alcoholism became steadily worse. I would drink during the day. I would call in sick. It became more and more expensive until one day, I misappropriated some funds from the Crowley Municipal Police Officer Association (CMPOA). I had been the treasurer.

I could cash checks with just my signature because the Crowley Municipal Police Officers Association had a one signature policy. Either the president or the treasurer could write a check.

I misappropriated about $950.00. I had intended to replace it before it was noticed, but the CMPOA President Gilford Richard got the bank statement and noticed the checks that I was writing for cash and reported it to Chief Gibson. Chief Gibson was willing to suspend me for ninety days with me paying restitution back to the CMPOA. When I told my wife, Linda, she asked me to resign to spare her and the children any more embarrassment and the constant notoriety that I would have gotten in the media by taking the suspension. She also wanted me to separate from her and to leave the house. I then talked to each one of the children, Kent, Jenifer, and Tracy individually explaining what I had done and that I was going to be gone until I could prove my trustworthiness again to their mother and that I could stop drinking alcohol.

I ask Chief Gibson if he would call a departmental meeting so that I could address the whole department. He did and I apologized for what I had done and for the embarrassment that I had caused the department. I was resigning effective immediately so not to cause them or my family any more embarrassment, and that I was going to repay the money that I had misappropriated, which I did.

CHAPTER 3

The Road to Recovery

And we know that in all things God works for the good of those who love him, who[a] have been called according to his purpose. (Rom. 8:28, NIV)

After I resigned from the Crowley Police Department, I went to stay a couple of days with an old friend and ex-neighbor Don Ledoux in Lake Arthur, Louisiana. I had contacted my brother who was the Pastor at the Methodist Church in Dequincy, Louisiana. He had a member of his church who was the Director of the Boise Southern 2/4 wood mill in Dequincy. He talked to him and he agreed to give me a job.

I moved to Dequincy and stayed at the Parsonage with my brother, Eddie, and his wife, Jackie, and their three sons, Dowd, Destin, and Derek. While there, I went to a psychologist at the Lake Charles Mental Health center for my alcoholism. He told me that he thought I was hypoglycemic and ask me to take the test to determine if I was. I did and I tested positive for it. He put me on a diet and for the whole time I was with Boise Southern I stayed sober.

I would come back to Crowley to see my wife, Linda, and three children on my days off. Linda could see the difference in me and agreed to give me another chance. So, on my days off, I would come back to Crowley and stay with the family. I had bought a small travel trailer while I was in Dequincy and moved from my brother's house to it and I would stay until my days off.

I continued at Boise Southern until the week before Christmas in 1979 when they started laying off and closing. I came back to

Crowley and moved the trailer to a camp ground in Longville, LA, where we used it as a camp.

About the middle of January 1980, I was hired by Western, an oil field Mud Company. After two weeks, there an opening with Dresser Atlas Wireline Service that paid a whole lot more. In fact, it is the only company that I know of that pays you two weeks in advance when you come to work, that I never had to pay back.

I went to work for Dresser Atlas the first of February 1980. The work was very hard and long, but it paid such a good salary that you got over it. We would stay on jobs anywhere from twelve hours to forty-eight hours per job. The hours that we worked, I was not able to keep to my diet so I started back to drinking. It never interfered with my work, but my wife Linda was not happy at all with it.

The shifts that we worked were seven days on two days off and seven days on and five days off. This is a modified shift of fourteen days on and seven off. On the five days, off I would get Linda and we would go on a trip all over the country. We even bought some acreage in Polk County, Tennessee, where we planned to retire someday.

I worked at Dresser Atlas until the end of September 1984 when the oil industry collapsed and they laid me off. They kept me on until the very last lay off. After they laid me off and about six others, they closed the shop in Rayne and moved the rest of the ones that were left to Lafayette. In six months, they sold out to Baker Hughes. There were thirteen lay off before that one. They paid me a three-month severance pay.

I was staying home and drawing unemployment, which is the hardest thing I have ever gone through. I was so ashamed to have to go to the unemployment office to apply for the unemployment check.

Linda had told me on the last trip we had taken that because I was drinking that she was not going back to the way things used to be. She had gone to Northside Assembly of God and had gotten save.

I wasn't drinking during the time I was unemployed, but because she had found so much peace with Jesus Christ, she wanted me to experience it too. Northside was having a retreat for married couples the weekend of October 25 to 26, 1984 at the Baptist Academy in

Eunice, LA, and she asked me if I would go with her, and I said yes, that I would. After the couple who was running the retreat had given their presentation, Associate Pastor Terrell Reed and his wife Debbie gave their testimony. It was almost Linda and my lives. He was an alcoholic and drug addict. Debbie had gotten saved and had taken Terrell to a revival where he had gotten saved and instantly, he was healed from alcoholism and drug addiction. While Terrell was talking, I heard the Holy Spirit tell me that this was the last time that I would have an opportunity to be saved. If I didn't accept Jesus as my savior, there wouldn't be another chance. I then accepted Jesus as my Savior, from that moment until today, I have never wanted a drink of alcohol.

Pastors Terrell and Debbie Reed

CHAPTER 4

Road to Redemption

For I know the plans I have for you," declares the Lord, "plans to prosper you and not to harm you, plans to give you hope and a future. (Jer. 29:11, NIV)

After several months of unemployment, I had really changed my life- style. I was a stay-at-home husband, so I did all the house work and cooking. I would also spend hours in reading the Bible and praying. When I had gotten saved, I had told a friend, Bill Jenkins, that I believed in the Holy Spirit, but I wasn't going to speak in tongues because I didn't believe you needed that to be filled with the Holy Spirit. Well, during one of the times that I was praying and reading the Bible, suddenly, I started speaking in a prayer language that I didn't recognize or understand, and have been using to speak to God when I didn't know in the natural how to pray.

God is so good that he supplies us with what we need even when we don't understand that we really do need them. He also does special things so that we know that it is him doing it and he is a loving caring Father. Like saving me on my forty-fifth birthday on October 25, 1984 so I would never forget the date. He would completely take away the desire for alcohol or drugs. He would restore what I let alcohol take away from me, my family, and my career in law enforcement.

During this early time, I had three months severance pay and I could draw unemployment compensation. That friend, Bill Jenkins, was the owner of the Kentucky Fried Chicken Franchise in Crowley and would bring the leftover Chicken and biscuits. I will always be grateful to him and his wife Loretta. I would also get pick up jobs from different people, like painting parking lot parking spaces at Kentucky Fried Chicken in Crowley, and spray washing Whitney Bank in Lafayette. Very humbling professions, but I was so grateful to get them because they always came at the exact time that I needed extra money, like the Whitney job coming two weeks before Christmas. This is probably the happiest time of my life because I had the opportunity to be able to communicate with God and to repair my marriage to Linda. It was probably the happiest time for her because she could see the change that God had done in my life and I became the husband that she always wanted and deserved.

If I had to name the greatest thing that I accomplished in my life it would be that she told me that I was her hero and that our three children had grown up to be highly successful God-fearing individuals who gave us six beautiful grandchildren, who, one day will all be the same successful children of God that their parents are. For her to have forgiven me for all that I had put her through and then tell me that I was her hero is just a God thing that leaves me breathless.

After about three months, a friend from the Dresser Atlas Days Keith Bourque got me an interview with Gearhart Industries, which was another wire line company. One of the bosses was Jim Gibson who had been my boss at Dresser Atlas. I was hired and went back to working in the oil industry. I will always be grateful to Keith and his wife Bonnie, for being such good friends; and to Jim for hiring me when I truly needed a job, unemployment compensation had run out, and there were no extensions.

About a year and six months or so, there was a men's retreat at the Acadia Baptist Academy in Eunice and I went with the men from Northside. The first night during the praise and worship part of the service, while singing "We are standing on Holy Ground," God spoke to me that if I stayed out of his way, he would make me Chief of Police of Jennings. I told Cleo Huval, who had become a friend at Northside Assembly of God. We had started attending the church at about the same time. He said well we will just believe it to be true.

Now there was not an opening for a Chief of Police in Jennings, LA, but God knew what was coming because about six months later, the Chief of Jennings resigned and an opening occurred. I took the Civil Service test, told my brother, who, at the time, was the pastor at Trinity United Methodist Church in Jennings, and that was it.

I was later told to report for an oral hearing. On the board was the City Attorney, Michael Cassady; Father Al Volpe, a Catholic Priest; a black political leader; and two others. I also took a psycho- logical test. I was recommended as the top choice and Mayor Jennifer Meyers appointed me Chief effective May 15, 1988. Mayor Meyers will always be special for taking the heat for hiring someone who had been an alcoholic and had misappropriated money from an organization that had trusted him. I hope that I have made her proud.

So, as the bible promised, "that where two or more are agree on anything that I will do," it became a reality. Cleo and his wife, Betty, will always have a special place in my life, prayers and thoughts. To all the people from Northside Assembly of God, in Crowley, Louisiana, especially Loyd and Patsy Singley, Terrell and Debbie Reed, Randy and Emma Trahan, Jim Girouard, and our Care Group: Floyd and Margie Harmon, Elwood and Gloria LeBlanc, Cleo and Betty Huval, and Sandra Henderson

CHAPTER 5

The Jennings Years

Take delight in the LORD, and he will give you the desires of your heart. (Ps. 37:4, NIV)

I started as Chief of Police of Jennings, Louisiana May 15, 1988. Mayor Jennifer Meyers, my wife, Linda, our daughter, Jenifer, and our son, Tracy, were there. City Attorney Michael Cassady swore me in. My brother, Eddie, prayed a prayer for me and the department. I will always be grateful for the role each of these played in my life especially Linda who gave me the best advice I ever got: "It's not who's right but what's right."

I had asked Mayor Meyers if she wanted to run the department or let me run it. She told me she had full confident in me to run the department. I assured her that I would keep her apprised of what we were doing. I will always be grateful for her support and trust.

The Sunday before I took office, Father Al Volpe had asked me if I would address the morning service at the Catholic Church. I agreed to it. He and I had discussed forming a Chaplin program for the Police Department. After I was sworn in I met with brother Eddie and Father Al and started the planning to get a Chaplin program started.

Father Al Volpe

During this time, Father Al Volpe and I went to several pastors in the community and formed a Chaplain Service for the Police Department. The original pastors were: Father AL; my brother, Rev. Eddie Morgan; Trinity United Methodist Church, Rev. Rickey Hebert; Jennings United Methodist Church, Mickey Istre, Pastor; and Mitchell Gott Associate, Pastor, Living Word Assembly of God, Jack Harris; First Church of Christ and Gerald Perkins. My brother Eddie left with in two years and Peter Harrington stayed for four years and Larry Maxwell replaced him.

This chaplain program produced six camps for indigent youth in Jennings. Where they could swim, learn different skills and have a relationship with the police who were the camp chaperon, 150 indigent youth went through the camp.

The chaplains were used as counselors to the policeman. They would also ride along with the police and were particularly helpful at family disturbance calls.

The Chaplains funded a program where if indigent people would come to one of the member churches, that church would send them to the police department, where we had made arrangement at several grocery stores, gas stations, and motels to except vouchers from the Police department. We would pay them off every first of the month. This was a separate fund from the city that were put into the

Chaplaincy program checking account. This fund also funded the camps that we put on for the indigent juveniles.

The chaplains were also there for the police officer's family. If any of them needed any type of help, the chaplains were always avail- able to them. They were also a sounding board for me. We would have a lunch at one of the restaurants that would give us a meeting room once a month, at which time, I would lay out any new program that I was going to start and they would tell me in which area the department could do better.

About two to three weeks after I was sworn in, an eighteen-wheeler over turned on 1-10 right by the Jennings exit. It had a cargo of dangerous chemicals. We were forced to evacuate about an eight-block area and divert traffic from 1-10 to US Highway 90. We did a credible job, but we were sorely unprepared. Took command of the law enforcement assets in the city because Louisiana law stated that if an incident affected a city, the Chief of Police of that city would be the lead law enforcement agency.

After that incident, within a couple of days, I called a departmental meeting. Set out a plan that would be followed for natural and man-made disasters like the one we had just had. This broke the department up into three twelve-hour shifts, the Red, the White, and the Blue team; each team had a specific time to report and what their duties were. I also gave instructions as to what I was to be called out on, murders, armed robberies, and assaults or batteries on officers. I told my shift supervisors that if I was called for anything other than these, then there were going to be one too many supervisors on the shift.

One of the first major crime cases that I worked on was a rape of an elderly white woman by an African American. This was on a Saturday morning, District Attorney Mike Cassady and I were playing golf when I received the call. I told Mike of the situation and that I had to leave, he said he would come with me since this was one of his first major cases since becoming DA.

The officers had gotten a description from an eyewitness that identified the suspect as the son of one of the men who worked at a service station about two blocks from the woman's house. Captain Steve Taylor and I interviewed the suspect, and the father told us

27

that his son was catching the bus at around eleven in the morning to go back to Texas.

Captain Taylor and I staked out the bus station starting about 10:45, and about eleven o'clock the suspect approached the bus as he was boarding. Captain Taylor and I identified ourselves and asked for his identification, and he showed us a driver's license that proved he was the subject we were looking for. We placed him under arrest. He later pleaded guilty.

The second major case was another rape of an African American female and by an African-American male. This happened before I became Chief. He was in the armed forces and was suspected of raping his girlfriend. When I became Chief, I started going through the cold case files and saw they had a suspect stationed in California. I sent a copy of the warrant to his base and a copy to the Kearns County California Sheriff's office. They arrested him and he waived extradition, so me and Officer Paul Menard drove to California to get him. The victim eventually dropped charges.

The third major case was a murder of a middle age trade school teacher. It was later found out that he was homosexual. We were developing leads, one pointed to one of his nephews. We couldn't locate him, so we put an all person bulletin (APB) on him as a person of interest.

We weren't developing any leads. I knew that Houston PD had a computer that if you put in pertinent facts into it like modus operando, it would give you some suspects who would fit the person or persons who did the Crime.

Lieutenant Kenneth Guidry and I went to Houston, and we talked to several detectives and they put the information we had into the computer. We went to dinner while the computer was g the files. When we came back, the computer gave four names as possible. At about the same time, I got a call from the Jennings Police Department. They told me that the New Mexico State Police had just apprehended four suspects in the car that belonged to the victim that we had mentioned in the APB. I ask for names and the dispatcher told me three names that matched three names that the computer had put out.

I called District Attorney Cassady and told him the situation and decided for Kenneth Guidry, a Jefferson Davis Parish Sheriff 's deputy, and I to fly out to Santa Cruz, New Mexico to interview the suspects. We interviewed each one separately and all four of them agreed to waive extradition. The next morning at the hearing to extradite, the judge and I had a conversation before the hearing. He had been stationed at Camp Beauregard, south of Alexandria, Louisiana and he had met some lawyers from Ville Platte that I knew. During the proceedings, the funniest thing that has ever happened in my career took place. The judge had giving all the suspects a copy of the affidavits and a copy of the APB that we had put out,

about maybe one of the perpetrators was a nephew of the victim.

When the main suspect read that, he jumped up and said, "Wait a minute, Judge, I'm not going back to Louisiana, I kill him, but I'm not kin to him."

The judge looked at me and said, "You want to subpoena me? That's a confession."

One other major event was the first Christmas that I was Chief of Police, a group of African Americans threw some beer cans and bottles at some of the police. After a brief confrontation, the police had the situation under control. The following weekend was New Years. I anticipated more trouble so I contacted the Sheriff of Jefferson Davis and Acadia Parish for additional manpower. I had told the mayor and the DA what I had intended on doing. I wanted to make a statement that what happened Christmas was not going to be tolerated.

We had a group meeting at the Jefferson Davis Parish Sheriff's detective office. There were ten deputies from Acadia Parish, ten deputies from Jefferson Davis Parish, and I had twenty City Policemen. I stressed that we weren't going to allow anyone to loiter or drink alcohol on the street. To tell them that once, then if they didn't move to cuff and stuff. Which meant arrest, cuff and bring to jail. They did exactly that, they arrested over one hundred people that night. From that night on until I left office, you could go down South Main in Jennings and not see anyone loitering or drinking on the street. Before that night, we were getting complaints every week.

Everything was going good. I had to shake up some of the staff because of the resentment to an outsider coming in. I reassigned the Secretary to the Chief of Police to a clerk position with the title of Secretary to the Chief of Police. I reassigned a dispatcher Eleanor Beall to secretary with the duties of Secretary to the Chief of Police. The Secretary to the Chief retired within a year of being reassigned and I promoted Eleanor to Secretary to the Chief with a considerable raise in salary. That was the best personnel decision that I have ever made.

Eleanor was priceless at being able to write policy, keep my schedule strait, handle my calls, and do payroll. I will always be grateful to her for the help in writing my correspondence with the IRS and the Louisiana State Treasurer's office to help the Jennings Police Department get into the Louisiana Municipal Police Officers Retirement System.

Secretary to the Chief Eleanor Beall

I would let her accompany me to most of the Chief of Police Association meetings so that she could meet other Secretaries to the Chief. She became very popular with the other secretaries and was eventually elected to President of the Secretary to the Chiefs of Police Association. 1 was so proud of her.

When she passed away in 2014, I was in shock because I had kept up with her and she had recovered from a foot injury and was doing fine. She was like a member of the family; she loved our - children and grandchildren as much as Linda and I did.

Through the help of David Fontenot, the Housing Authority Director, we obtained an apartment in the highest crime ridden housing project and the police department could open a sub-station, the Peter Street station. We could reduce calls from the projects from fifteen to thirty per month to two per month. The drug dealers and other troublemakers were out of the area within three months. That substation is still open today. We used this for the officers assigned to the high crime area in the south main section of Jennings. We were also able to stop the littering, loitering, and drug dealings in this area. I had put Captain Shelton Breaux as commander of Peter Street Station. He, and the officers who were assigned at the Southside zone, would work out of that office. They had a kitchen where they could keep coffee and any food they wanted to heat up. It was also a place where the residents of the housing projects could come and visit and drink coffee or get cold soft drinks out of the machine or snacks out of the snacks machine.

The most important program we instituted was the PASIN (Police Assisting Students in Need). With the help of Jefferson Davis Parish School superintendent, James Whitford, we could put a resource officer in every school in Jennings starting in the elementary grades.

Patrolman Robert Guillory with Elementary
students at the Jennings Elementary School.

We started with Patrolman Robert Guillory. He was an exceptional PASIN officer. He had a remarkable repose with the children. He was well respected by the teachers and the principle. He stayed in that position for two years until he thought himself more important then what he was. I would let the officers talk to the press about cases that they were directly involved in. Well, the Jennings Daily News had asked if they could do a story on the PASIN program. I authorized for him to interview with them since he was doing such an outstanding job. I was thinking that he was going to talk about the success of the program, like getting two students who were making failing grades to become honor roll students. Instead of this, he got off into politics and made the statement that he was more popular than the mayor was. This was on a Friday and it made the Sunday paper.

When I called him in on Monday for him to explain why the interview had turned political, he became arrogant restating that he was doing such a good job that he was more popular than the mayor, and that if he wanted to, he could run and beat him. Well, I thought that since he wanted to be Mayor that he should be close to the Mayor's office to learn what the job was. I reassigned him to a traffic assignment working traffic at the corner where the Mayor's office was. He lasted about three days and resigned. I really hated to lose him, but he didn't understand that police work was a team effort and no one was more important than the team and how the public reacted to the police. He was the best PASIN officer that I had, but others were just as capable and all did excellent jobs.

Jennings, LA Police Captain Steve Taylor, Patrolman
Robert Guillory and Chief Carroll Morgan

I would say that the worst decision I made as Chief of Police was to hire Philip Karam. I had known him from the time that he had spent being Wildlife and Fishery Officer. I knew he was a good Wildlife and Fishery Officer, he told me he had a drinking problem from having flash backs from Vietnam, but it had not affected his job.

33

He had been wounded in Vietnam and had lost a leg. He had a prosthetic leg. He would sometimes have trouble with the stump and must go to the VA to get attention for it. He once broke the prosthetic leg making an arrest. But that was the only real medical problems I had with him. When he would think that the depression-was or the urge to drink was getting too bad, I would send him   to a psychologist in Lafayette. He would do outpatient treatment with Philip. The psychologist always told me that he didn't think that Philip would be violent or have a drinking problem if he could get to the psychologist when he needed too. Kenneth Guidry and his wife were best friends with Philip. What made Philip crack and kill both, we will never know. Philip never made a statement. As far as I know, I don't think there was anything between Officer Burt LeBlanc; he was just the officer that responded.

Kenneth Guidry was also a Vietnam veteran that is why he could understand Philip Karam. He was sometimes hard to take because he seemed little too overbearing and flamboyant. He was very cocky, but deep inside, when you got to know him, he was a caring person and an excellent officer. I got to know him well because I took him to a Hostage Negotiators School put on by the Texas Rangers and the Hostage Negotiators Association of Texas. This was right after the David Koresh case at Waco, Texas where the ATF and Koresh's clan had a shootout, and several of the Koresh group were burned to death or shot to death.

Several ATF agents were also killed and wounded. We got to see the films and the original conversation between Koresh and the Waco, Texas dispatcher. He and I had a week to get to know each other. I always had great respect for Kenny. He will always be missed by me.

Burt LeBlanc was one of the proudest hires that I have made over my career. He was a young officer who was always curious and wanting to learn. He had unlimited potential. It was such an empty feeling when I got the call about what had happened. They said that Philip Karam had been to Kenneth Guidry's house from early that afternoon and that Philip had been drinking and wanted to drive a car that Kenny had let Philip drive because he had lost everything. When Philip couldn't get the car, he got mad and left the house and walked back to his apartment. He came back later and killed Kenny and his wife. Kenny's wife before she died called 911and told them that she and her husband had been shot and that he was dead, and that Philip Karam was the one who did the shooting.

Patrolman Burt LeBlanc and Chief Carroll Morgan when Patrolman LeBlanc graduated from Basic Training.

Officer Burt LeBlanc got the call to go to Kenny's house; and when he walked up to the door, he was shot and killed instantly. My son, Tracy, who is a Louisiana State Policeman was assigned to Troop D. This troop covers the Jennings area. Tracy was at the time assigned to the detective division. He spotted him in a field a little way from Kenny's house and he arrested him.

Captain Steve Taylor had been Chief of Police of Jennings twice before I got there; both times, he voluntarily giving up the job because of personal reasons. He was very smart and capable, but unable or wouldn't make decisions on his own. I assigned him to oversee the patrol division. He did a capable job of following orders, but I can't recall him bringing any new programs to me.

Captain Breaux, he was very flamboyant and cocky, but he related well with the residence in the Peter Street station area. He made contacts and friends that were very useful for intelligent purpose He was not a self-starter; you continuously had to ask for reports from him.

Sgt. Terry Guillory, very capable officer, but sometimes, he wanted to be a clown. It got him into trouble one time with me. He was riding in my unit and he started cursing. I told him that I didn't curse and would appreciate if he didn't. He would not stop using some words I found offensive, so I stopped the unit about a mile from the police station and put him out of the unit and made him walk back to the station. I didn't have that problem with him again, he still talks about it every time I see him. I replaced Officer Robert Guillory (no relations) with Terry as a PASIN Officer.

District Attorney, Michael Cassady; I will always be grateful to him for his trust in me to get me through the oral review board. I will always treasure his friendship while I was Chief and since I have been Chief. He has always been highly professional with me, both as City Attorney and District Attorney.

Wendell Miller was District Attorney when I was appointed Chief of Police. He was a very competent District Attorney; and after being elected District Judge, he is one of the top three judges that I have worked with.

Mayor Meyers made the decision to not run again for Mayor, so the City Clerk, Greg Marcantel, ran and won. I asked him if he wanted to keep me as Chief of Police or whether he would like to hire his own. He told me he was satisfied with the job I was doing. I asked him if he wanted to keep the same arrangement that Mayor Meyer's and I had or did he want to run the department. He told me he wanted to keep the same arrangement. So I did. He would have a staff meeting every Monday morning, and I would brief him about what the police had done and apprise him of any changes we were contemplating to make.

During Mayor Marcantel's time as mayor, we made arrangment with his permission with the State of Louisiana Department of Corrections to hold state prisoners in the City Jail for $21.00 a day per prisoner. I started with fifteen prisoners. That is $21.00 X 15=

$315.00 a day or $2,205.00 a week. It cost $5.75 to feed, house, and provide security or a profit of $309.75 a day or $2126.25 a week or $110,565.00 a year.

Another thing that the department hadn't kept up with was police training. I contacted Dean McCameron with LSU; I told him that I needed to contact Mike Toupousis who was running the LSU Law Enforcement in Service Training. Mike was a retired FBI Agent whom I had known from going to the LSU Juvenile Officers School. He was more than happy to help with in-service training. We had a different subject that they taught every six months. We kept this up the whole time I was Chief of Police. I would also send some of the officers to specialized schools.

Somewhere in the latter part of 1994, Linda started getting sick. She was tired with no energy at all. We went to several doctors, but none of them could diagnose what was wrong. At the same time, I too was feeling terrible, face swollen, and my memory was gone. I couldn't remember what I was doing. I would get in the car and start driving and then ask Linda where I was going.

My daughter's friend, Debbie Cormier, got Linda into see Dr. Richard Broussard, a Gastroenterologist from Lafayette, Louisiana and got me into see a cardiologist Dr. Lester Ducote, Jr. As soon as Dr. Ducote looked at me, he said you have thyroid problems. So he sent me down to the lab to do blood work and the results was that my thyroid reading was 93 microunits per milliliter. The normal is -0.4 to 4.2 microunits per milliliter for adults. Dr. Ducote told me that he didn't know how I was operating. He put me on thyroid medicine and I haven't had any problems since.

Mayor Marcantel and I seemed to have had a good relationship; but sometime in April 1995, he called me to his office and asked me to resign, and that he wanted to have someone else take the department in another direction than the way I was leading it. He was getting complaints from some of the officers. I was devastated. I was hurt so badly because I knew the Lord had given me that job and I felt that Mayor Marcantel was taking it away that I broke down. I told him I wouldn't resign. So, two days later, he fired me. I was accused of using my city computer for personal use on city time. I had, but not on city time. There was a Civil Service hearing and they up held the firing. I had asked my lawyer to appeal but he let the time elapse.

I have come to realize that this was a God thing because after I got fired, Linda really got sick and Dr. Broussard had a Surgeon Dr. Stephens do exploratory surgery and they found that she had contacted Hepatitis C and that she had Cirrhosis of the Liver. They suspect it came from one blood transfusion that she was given in 1975 because she had lost some blood from the radiation they given her to cure cervix cancer. During this time, she had several stays in the hospital and I had to be with her all the time. Dr. Broussard got us an appointment with the transplant personnel at Baylor Hospital in Dallas, Texas.

She was put on the transplant list. About nine to ten months later, she was called to Dallas, that she was the next one in line for a transplanted liver. Baylor Hospital had a hotel in the hospital. When Linda was put on the transplant list, the room cost $25.00 a night. By the time she was called, the room rate had increased double to $50.00 a night. I stayed with her for a week, but I had to go back to work. While I was there, our Pastor Jeff Ogg from Bethel Temple Assembly of God in Baton Rouge, Louisiana call to ask how things were going. During the conversation, I happened to mention that the room rate had doubled and that we had only saved for $ 25.00 a night, but that we would be able to make it. A couple of nights later, he called me to tell me that someone in the church wanted to donate $2,500.00 to us. He asked me if I would accept it. I told him sure. The donor wanted to be anonymous and I still don't know who they were.

CHAPTER 6

The Department of Correction Years

⁴Rejoice in the Lord always. I will say it again: Rejoice! 5 Let your gentleness be evident to all. The Lord is near. 6 Do not be anxious about any- thing, but in every situation, by prayer and petition, with thanksgiving, present your requests to God. 7 And the peace of God, which transcends all understanding, will guard your hearts and your minds in Christ Jesus. (Phil. 4:4–7)

I began my career at the Department of Correction June of 1195. Bill Jenkins had sold the Kentucky Fried Chicken franchise in Crowley and had moved to Baton Rouge, Louisiana and had gone to work with Elyan Hunt Correctional Center in St. Gabriel, Louisiana. When he had found out that I had been fired from the Jennings Police Department, he called me and told me there where openings at the Hunt Correctional Center for transportation officers. I took the civil service test and was hired. I would commute back and forth from Jennings and stay at the officers' quarters at Hunt Correctional Center when I was on duty and go back to Jennings on my days off. It was while I was home on my days off that my daughter's friend, Debbie, got me an appointment with Dr. Lester Ducote from Lafayette, Louisiana. He diagnosed me with thyroid problems. I started taking the medicine and within a few days I was feeling a one hundred percent better.

I continued to commute from Jennings for about two months while we looked for an apartment in the Baton Rouge area. We finally found one in Baton Rouge. Linda had progressively gotten worse health-wise and was of little help moving, but my great nephew, Brent Jones, helped by driving the U-Haul truck for me.

We stayed in the apartments for about a year when a friend, Kirk Kanatani, from our church who was a developer and financier talked to me. We were talking about Linda and me wanting to buy a house. He told me he would look around for land and that he would build us a house for ten percent above cost. We found some property in Prairieville, Louisiana. We bought the land for $20,000.00 and before we could build, it increased in value to $40,000.00. We started building in May and was supposed to be in the new house July 1 when our lease at the apartment expired. When July came, they were not through. We moved into the house the night of the July1, and Linda would have to leave in the daytime so the inspector wouldn't know. We did for about a week until it was inspected.

This was another God thing. We didn't have any money for a down payment. He got a bank to finance the construction cost and a lending company to give us a loan with no down payment. I had drawn the plans for the house and Linda and I dedicated that house to God. We truly enjoyed that home. My current wife and I sold it to a young sweet couple in 2010 who I am sure are blessed. They have done a lot of improvements and have really enhanced it.

I had made arrangement through Thurmond "Scooter" McMorris my Lieutenant, with Assistant Warden Mariann Leger and Warden Marty Lindsey to work seven days on and seven days off. I would work from Monday thru Sunday.

On the next Sunday night, I called her and asked her if she wanted me to come that night or if she wanted me to wait until Monday. She told me to wait until Monday that she was feeling good. At two o'clock in the morning, I get a call from her telling me that they had just called her and she was going to the hospital that they had a liver for her. So I called my daughter, Jenifer, who was living in Lafayette; my son, Tracy, who lived in Westlake, Louisiana; and my son, Kent, who was living in The Woodlands, Texas. Within an hour, Tracy and I met at Jenifer's and we were on the road to Dallas. Kent left from The Woodlands. Kent beat us to Dallas and did see his mother before the operation. We arrived while she was in recovery. As soon as we saw her, there was that old glow on her face and in her eyes. Before the transplant, she looked like walking death, her weight was about 100 lbs. on a 5'10" frame. After the surgery, she was her beautiful self again. Another miracle that God performed.

I want to especially thank the people who made the transplant possible. Linda had to stay twelve weeks in an apartment that Baylor has for transplant patients. Someone would have to stay with her the whole time. I could only stay one week at a time. The following people stayed the other six weeks, Linda's mother, Margorie Wilmoth Marx, Linda's sisters, Alice North and Ellen Bush, my daughter, Jenifer Carriere, and our friend, Fran Gilbert, who stayed two weeks. A special thanks to the husbands Don North, Britt Bush, Scott Carriere, and my special friend, Harlan "Gil" Gilbert. She lived a normal life for six and one half years. The best six and one half years of our marriage.

We found that faith in God, our family and each other were the most important things. That each moment was special and we had to make the best out of each of them. That nothing was guaranteed. That we are here for such a brief-moment that each minute counts. We learned that through faith in Jesus, we could get through anything. That total healing may not come on earth but total healing will come when we meet him. We learned to be happy no matter what we face because his Grace is sufficient for all our needs.

On December 31, 2004, she passed away while in hospice care at our home in Prairieville, Louisiana. I will always be grateful to Warden Lindsey, Warden Leger, Thurman "Scooter" and Dawn McMorris, Bill and Loretta Jenkins, Glenn and Rita Passmore, Chuck and Sue Pampell, Larry and Suzette Freeman, Paul and Vi Balto, Vernon and Connie Dodd, Bill and Frankie Courtney, Wade and Lauren David, Jimmie Meeks and Kirk Kanatani for the support and love that they showed me during the time of need and after.

On February 4, 2005, I had an angioplasty heart test that showed that I had ninety percent blockage in two of my heart arteries and that I would need open-heart surgery. My son, Tracy, told the Doctor that he had better put me in the hospital now or he would never see me again. So I consented to the operation. At 7:30 in the morning, they did the operation and I was in the recovery room at eleven and in intensive care room at two in the afternoon.

I was out on sick leave for about four weeks, and then went on light duty for another six weeks at hunt running the control center in the block. I went back into transportation after I came off light duty.

The only exciting or unusual things that happened while I was at Hunt was that as I was searching an inmate to shackle him up to transport to the East Baton Rouge Parish Courthouse, I found a make shift knife in his shoe. I notified his housing captain; and when I got to the East Baton Rouge Courthouse, I told the deputies there. He needed to be separated from the other prisoners and to be kept restrained. There was no other incident with this inmate.

The other one happened about a month after I was hired. Hunt had a policy that if anyone tried to escape that we had to fire a warning shot before shooting the escapee.

One of the cell block inmates, who were the worse on the compound, as I was restraining him to take to the hospital, he asks me, "Mr. Morgan, if I run, are you going to fire a warning shot?"

I looked him straight in the eye and as serious as a heart attack, I called him by his first name and said, "Yes, but you want hear it."

He looked at me and said, "Mr. Morgan I believe you." I told him, "Believe it."

I never had any trouble out of him.

The only other inmate to try me was one, who, as we were leaving Earl K Long Charity Hospital in Baton Rouge, started to walk faster than the other inmates and tried to get to a corner of another building so he could break if he wanted to. I told him to stop. He did then he started backing up and I unsnapped my holster.

He said, "What are you going to do? Take your gun out and shoot me."

I told him, "Take one more step and we will both know."

He didn't and I didn't have any more trouble with any other inmates.

Linda had left me some life insurance; and my son, Tracy, asked me to check into whether I could buy some of my police time into the state retirement system. I checked into it and found out I could, and I had enough money to buy five years, which gave me fifteen years.

After the open-heart operation, I decided that I would retire October 1, 2005. I took three months' term leave and effectively retired July 1, 2005.

After I retired, I stayed in Prairieville. I would take trips to visit old friends all over the country. I took a trip to Hawaii with my grandson, Allen Carriere. He had just finished his second tour of duty in Iraq with the Louisiana National Guard.

I went white water rafting with two of my grandsons, Timothy Morgan and Michael Carriere, in North Carolina.

I was really enjoying myself. I was still attending Bethel Temple Assembly of God. I had been elected to the church board. I was not really looking for anyone. One day, as we were eating after church, my friends Suzette and Larry Freeman told that they were praying for me to meet someone so that I could remarry. I asked them not to, but they did.

About six months later, I met a lady from Crowley, Helen Joyce Broussard Trahan. She was a Vice President of Bank of Commerce and Trust, Company, Crowley, Louisiana. She went to an Assembly of God Church. She went to the church I used to go to, Northside Assembly of God, Crowley.

About six months, later we were married, May 19, 2007. She has three beautiful daughters; Pamela Dupont, Rene Lastrappe, and Paula Bouillion. She continued to work for two years then retired in 2009. We live in Crowley.

HELEN JOYCE BROUSSAR MORGAN,
AUGUST 14, 1942-10-18-2022

In 2012, she had two mini stokes. In 2015, she was diagnosed with Alzheimer's disease. She is being treated by a doctor associated with the Nance Alzheimer's Clinic at Methodist Hospital in Houston, Texas.

This is in God's hands. She can still function. We can go out and eat, go to church, and to our church's growth group. We are taking it day by day. Some days, she gets confused. She doesn't know where she is or who we are. Then other days, she knows a good amount.

This is another experience that draws you close to the bosom of Jesus. I pray constantly to him that he gives me wisdom, patients, and compassion. Without his grace and love, I would not be able to cope. His grace is sufficient for all my needs.

I thank God for Pamela, Rene, and Paula; and my children Kent, Jenifer, and Tracy; without their support, it would be almost impossible.

Helen Joyce Morgan passed away the morning of October 18,2022 at the age of 80 years from complication of Alzheimer's.

CHAPTER 7

Police Public Relations

> Therefore, there is now no condemnation for those who are in Christ Jesus, 2 because through Christ Jesus the law of the Spirit who gives life has set you[a] free from the law of sin and death. (Rom. 8:1–2, NIV)

I am writing this chapter because of the attacks on the police that have occurred during the past six years. First, let me dispel the idea that police use their weapons indiscriminately. Most officers go their entire career without firing their weapon in the line of duty.

To restore confidence between police departments and the public that they serve, there must be a short term and long term four prong program that is aimed at: education, community policing, trust, and a justice system that works.

The First Prong is Education

Police departments must recruit and train officers who want to be public school PASIN (Police Assisting Students in Need) Officers. All schools should have at least three PASIN Officers per school.

The primary duty of the PASIN Officer is to help the problem student with his/her homework and his/her discipline and to form a bond between the officer and student. This means training the police officers in tutoring and educational counseling skills.

Because the PASIN Officer will be called on to help with discipline, they must be well trained with martial arts and self-defense skills so that they can control disruptive students. He must also be an expert marksman with a hand gun in case of a potential or active shooter on school grounds.

The PASIN Officer must undergo psychological and physical exams every 6 months. The PASIN officers should be uniformed officers except one that should be in plain clothes.

The uniform officers would be used as a deterrent and to familiarize the students and faculty that the policeman is the good guy and not someone to be afraid of or someone who is out to get them. The reason for the plain clothes officers is for safety, intelligence gathering, and familiarizations reasons. If an individual wants to cause havoc, they would try to take out the uniformed officers first. Every public school should have these PASIN Officers. Starting:

first year in the elementary schools, the second year in the middle schools, the third year in the junior high schools, and fourth year in high schools.

This way, in twelve years, you will have a student, who, for every year, would have developed a positive relationship with the police. In that twelve years, you will be three years with no police presents in some of the schools. The schools could modify this by starting all the schools at the same time. This would take the risk of older students rebelling against the discipline that police would natural provide.

The Second Prong is Community Policing

By having the housing authority provide a free apartment for a police substation in every housing project that the city runs that are in high crime and truancy areas. These apartments should be well staffed with well trained police officers twenty-four hours a day.

They should be well trained in the law and departmental policy. They should be well trained in self-defense, martial arts, and expert with all types of firearms, tear gas, and Taser. They should have extensive training in public relations and race relations. They should be well disciplined, they should make friends with the folks in the other apartments, they must always be professional, and they must follow departmental policies without exceptions. Some of the office staff should also be trained in tutoring and educational counseling.

There should be a strong enough force to command respect and to be able to carry out the goals of the department to curb crime, create trust, and to bring tranquility to the work area.

By having neighborhood precincts in the Housing Authority, this should give the police a base to work from within the community. It should be staffed with either a deputy chief or some rank high enough to make decisions without going through the bureaucracy.

Each station house should have an intelligence unit that should be cross-trained with Homeland Security, Immigration & Border Patrol. Immigration laws ought to be strictly enforced and close coordination with the Border Patrol should be maintained to speedily get the illegal immigrants adjudicated.

Strict transparency should be maintained. Any wrong doings should be investigated immediately and proper punishment, if any, rendered. Unscheduled inspections should be held periodically.

The Third Prong is Trust

The first prong is a long-term of three to fifteen years. The second prong should bring results in six to nine months. Both projects are geared to bring trust back into the neighborhoods that need police presence the most.

By putting an adequate police presence in the high crime areas and having a physical presence in the actual housing facilities, the police can develop one on one relationship that will eventually lead to trust. The citizens of the neighborhood will come to realize they can live in peace without having unruly people terrorizing the neighborhood.

They will realize the police are just like they are; they have families that they want the best for and want them to live in a safe environment.

The PASIN program in school is geared to help the student that needs tutoring, or needs someone to teach them discipline, to help them with their studies, and to counsel them in to making good and right choices.

By having these PASIN Officers in the early life of the student, we can change attitudes and perceptions of the police. The trained officers in the substation could reinforce this after school hours.

The funding for these programs can be provided by all three agencies. The Housing Authority furnishes the facilities and utilities for the substations. The school boards can fund the PASIN officer for nine months, and the police department for three months. When the school is out, the PASINS officer will do in-service training. The police department would pay the salary expenses. The education department would furnish the training. To further reinforce trust, all officers of the department shall have a body camera on the entire time the officer is on duty.

The Fourth Prone is to Have a Justice and Correction System that Works

Have a nonviolent juvenile facility in each congressional district. If a juvenile gets sentenced to those facilities, they would have to either get a high school degree, GED, or a trade apprentice certificate before they are released or age twenty-one. There could be separate housing for female and male students but only one school system.

There should be two juvenile facilities for violent juveniles one for females and one for males.

Have a nonviolent first offender minimum-security prisons in each congressional district. Only nonviolent first offending adults will be allowed.

These prisons would be staffed with teachers, tradesmen, family counseling (that would be voluntary for the families to attend), and drug rehab professionals along with profession Department of Correction Personnel.

If the offenders have a drug offense, they must attend and complete a drug rehab program.

This facility should have a high school diploma or GED program, so that sentencing requires that they either must have a high school diploma or equivalent or either or have completed a trade course certifying them as an apprentice (painter, plumber, electrician, carpenter, welder, and etc.) before they are to be released.

They would be sentenced to an indeterminate time. The faster they get their education and complete the drug rehab successfully, the faster they get out. Have a work release program that they would have to complete before being release totally free back onto street.

Take a percentage of their wages to pay for all of this. This gives them some skin in the game.

Some violent first offenders and second offenders would go to medium prison that will be in a combination of two adjourning Congressional Districts closes to their homes.

These should be hard labor camps, such as farming, maintenance, and etc.

Violent first offenders, third offenders, and all others would be sentenced to one of two maximum-security male prisons and one maximum-security female prison. They would be taught skills that would benefit the intuition. Very few of these would ever see the outside again.

But if we are to really change things, we must come to grips with the core problem that is affecting our inner cities and even our rural area. The problem of one parent homes. Churches and schools should be teaching the benefits of abstinence from sex until after marriage. Personal responsibility for one's actions should be a para- mount teaching starting in the earliest grades. Every child, no matter the circumstance, should have the choice of what school to attend. Teachers should be tested periodically to make sure they are qualified to teach.

But most of all, we need a Christian revival, another Billy Graham or John Wesley, to preach the gospel of Jesus Christ and the Cross.

You have a testimony, you have a story. Please share it because you never know who needs to hear it. Terrell and Debbie Reed shared theirs and I am a life that was changed.

IN MEMORY OF MY SON
TRACY A. MORGAN

My son, Tracy, died of a heart disease that no one knew about January 10, 2017. He died while this book was being published. He was a Christian who loved his God. He loved his wife of 22 years and his children. He was a loved and was a loving son and brother. He served five years with the United States Marine Corp some during Desert Storm, three years with the Lake Charles, Louisiana Police Department and 28 years with the Louisiana State Police. He was a crisis negotiator serving as Executive Director of the Louisiana Crisis Negotiators and was serving on the Board of Directors at the time of his death. I didn't write enough about him in this book. I will try to write another book about him and his impact on the lives he came in contact.

ABOUT THE AUTHOR

Born October 25, 1939, Crowley, Louisiana

Twenty-four years' experience, Patrol Officer to Chief of Police Graduated from LSU Basic Training

Graduated Second in his class LSU Juvenile Officers Academy

600 Hours of LSU and FBI In-Service Training schools

Municipal Police Officers Association of Louisiana, Past -President

Louisiana Chief of Police Association, Board of Directors, Legislative, Sick Leave, Union Relations Committees.

Member of the LSU Law Enforcement Academy Advisory Board

Associate member of American Academy of Forensic Science. Member of the Texas Association of Hostage Negotiators

Helped to get full funding Police Supplemental Pay for Louisiana City Police

Helped to get funding of LSU Law Enforcement Institute Ten-year Louisiana Department of Corrections Officer

Graduated from Basic Academy for Correctional Officers, Angola State Penitentiary

Elayn Hunt Correctional Center, Officer of the Month

Presidey of Louisiana Ready Group, a nonprofit group who are missionaries and advocates for Law Enforcement.

Presidet of Ready Louisiana LLC a House of Worship security consultaing company.